Glossary

F 95

G 104

H 109

I 116

P.....................154

.io (websites)
/ajo /
Noun
Noun:io
Definition

1. The term io means the Indian Ocean
2. The .io domain is a more generic top level
   domain

Related words: Org, .com etc.

24th High
/24 haj/

Adjective
Adjective: 24 high
Definition

1. This refers to the highest prices in the
   stock in the last 24 hours

Related words: 24 lows

24th low

/24 lo/

Adjective
Adjective: 24th low
Definitions

1. This refers to the lowest prices in a stock market in the last 24 hours

Related words: 24 high

2fa Security

/2fa sɪkjʊrəti/

Noun
Noun: 2fa security
Definition

2. This is a security process in which the user provides 2 authenticating factors to ensure that only the legitimate users can have access to the secured data.

Acronym: 2-factor authentication.
Related words: 2 step verification

51% attack
Definitions

/51 ətæk/

Verb

Verb: 51% attack

1. This is a flaw in the BTC design which
   allows anyone with the majority of
   network hash rate to have substantial
   control of the public ledger.

Related words: hash rate

Abescrow

/ ab escrow/

Noun
Noun: ab escrow
Definition

1. An anonymous bitcoin-based secure escrow service

Related words: escrow

Acceptance policy

/ ǝkˈsɛptǝns ˈpɒlɪsi /

Adjective
Adjective: acceptance policy
Definition

1. This refers to a shift in the traditional policy of a company or an organization that had begun accepting cryptocurrency. E.g. cheaper pricing against traditional currencies.

Related words: security

Access coin
/ **asəletər** /

Noun
Noun: oscillator
Definition

1. This is used to make the purchase of bitcoin through Google check out and requires Facebook for a second-factor authentication

Related words:

Accelerator/ Decelerator
/ æksɛləretər /decelerator/
Noun:
Noun: accelerator/ decelerator
Definition

1. This is a technical indicator that measures acceleration and deceleration of a recent market driving force
2. This is an early warning signal which changes direction before any change in the driving force, which in turn will change direction before the change in prices

Adaptive difficulty
/ ədæptɪv skelɪŋ/

verb
Verb: Adaptive scaling
Definition

1. This is a bitcoin protocol change proposal with the goal of letting the typical time intervals from one block to the next adjust smoothly to prevailing network latency.

Related words:

Address
/ædrɛs/

Noun
Noun: address
Definition

1. This refers to a possible destination for a digital currency payment.
2. It is a string of special numbers for accepting or receiving payments from either clients, investors, exchangers and even merchants of digital currencies

Related words: Bitcoin address, public address, private address

ADX/DMS

/ adx / dms/

Noun

Noun: ADX/DMS

1. ADX/DMS is an indicator that uses three inputs to analyzing the strength and direction of a price trend.

Related words:

Affiliate

/ əfiliet/

Verb
Verb: affiliate
1. The term affiliate is a kind of relationship between companies in which one of the companies owns less than a majority of the other company's stock
2. The term affiliate refers to the degree of ownership a parent company is holding in a different company

Related words: Referral

Affiliate Code
/ əfɪliet kod/

Noun

Noun: affiliate code

1. Affiliate code is a tracking code that is used to register and assign conversions and clicks in affiliate marketing.

2. Affiliate code is a unique code of 3-5 letters and a key mechanism for registering clients referred by affiliates

Relate words: nil

Algorithms
/ ælgərɪðəm /

Noun

Noun: algorithms

1. This refers to set rules used in accomplishing tasks in specified steps

2. Algorithms are specific sets of clearly defined instructions aimed to carry out specific tasks or process.

Related words: Algorithmic trading,

Altcoin
/altcoins/

Noun

Noun: altcoins

1. Altcoins simply means alternative coins
2. Altcoins refers to all other types of cryptocurrencies except bitcoin.

Related words:litecoin,eutherum,etc.

AMD cards
/amd kards/

Noun

Noun: amd cards

Anonymous Transactions
/ənanəməs trænzækʃənz/

Verb

Verb: anonymous transactions

1. This refers to the sending and receiving of digital currencies without giving any personal identifying information
2. This is the usage of a different address for a different transaction to prevent chances of a possible attack

Related words

Arbitrage
/arbətraʒ/

Verb

Verb: arbitrage

1. Arbitrage refers to a process by which a person trades instantly one or more pairs of currencies for a risk-free profit

Related words:

Ascending Triangle
/ əsɛndɪŋ trajæŋgəl /

Noun

Noun: ascending triangle

1. This is a bullish chart pattern used in technical analysis that is easily recognizable and is usually found amid a period of integration within an uptrend or an upsurge.

Related words: continuation pattern, descending triangle

Asia Nexgen

/ eʒə nɛksdʒɛn/

Noun

Noun: Asia NexGen

Definitions

1. This is an exchange trading platform for buying and selling bitcoins in traditional currencies around the world. E.g. USD, EURO, AUD, CHF ETC.

Related words:

ASIC

/ ˈeɪsɪk/

Noun

Definition

1. A computer chip created to perform one specific function, and only that function.
2. This is an integrated circuit, which is created and customized for intended uses.

Abbreviations: Application-specific integrated circuit

Related words:

Asymmetric Key Algorithm
/**asymmetric** ki ælgərɪðəm/

Noun

Noun: asymmetric key algorithm

1. This refers to the use public and private keys to encrypt and decrypt data. Such keys are simply, a large combination of numbers and letters that have been paired together, and are not identical.

Related word: asymmetric cryptography, public key cryptographs.

Autobot
/ *Autobot*/

Noun

Noun: Autobot

Definition

1. This is a cryptocurrency software that allows for the automation of marketing strategies.

2. This is an application that trades on behalf of a user using C.A.T algorithm

Related words: crypto trader, cryptographic automatic trader.

Average True Range
/ *æʋərɪdʒ tru rendʒ* /

Adjective
Adjective: Average True Range
Definition

1. An average true range is a volatility indicator which basically provides an indication of price trend or the degree of price volatility

Abbreviations: *ATR*

Related words: average range

Awesome Oscillator
/ asəm asəletər/
Adjective:
Adjective: Awesome Oscillator
Definition

1. This is an indicator used in measuring market momentum,

2. This is used to calculate a 34 period and 5-period simple moving averages

Abbreviations: *AO.*

Related words: simple moving averages etc.

B

Bag holding
/ bæg holdɪŋ/
Verb
Verb: Bag holding
Definition

1. Bag holding the process of holding a position in a stock which decreases in value until it has no worth or value
2. Bag holding is the possession of stock which deteriorates in value

Related words

Bear
/ bɛr /
Noun
Noun: Bear
Definition

1. A bear is an investor is one who attempts to profit from a decline in price because he/she believes that a particular security or market is headed downwards

Related words: bearish, bear closing

Bearish
/ bɛrɪʃ /
Noun
Noun
Definition
1. This is a term used to describe a market chart that shows or indicates a rise in market prices.

Related words: bear, bear closing, bullish e.t.c

Bear closing
/ bɛr klozɪŋ/
Verb
Verb: bear closing
Definition

1. This is a strategy designed to profit from falling prices of commodities or currencies in order to close bear positions
Related words

Bear Trap

/ bɛr træp /
Verb
Verb: bear trap
Definition

1. A bear trap is a manipulation of stock and commodities by investors in order to fool investors into thinking the upward trend in value has stopped and may deteriorate;

2. Bear trap is a false signal that signifies that rising trends of a stock or index has reversed when it has not.

Related words: bear closing, bear

Bitcoin
/ bitcoin /
Noun
Noun: bitcoin
Definition
1. A Bitcoin is a type of digital currency in which encryption techniques are used to regulate the generation of units of currency and to verify financial transactions without the need for a central bank.

2. Bitcoin is an online currency made of processed data blocks used for online, brick and mortar purchases.

3. Bitcoin is a currency that requires that transactions be made by middlemen thereby cutting off banks.

Related words: cryptocurrency, digital currency, virtual currency

Bitcoin Price Index (BPI)
/ bitcoin prajs ɪndɛks /
Adjective
Adjective: bit coin price index

1. This is an index number expressing the level of bitcoin prices relative to the level of the prices of bitcoin during an arbitrary chosen based periods, indicating changes in prices of bitcoin from one period to another.

2. This represents an average of bitcoin prices across leading global exchanges that meet criteria specified by the XBP

3. BPI, gathers information from the information largest most influential Bitcoin exchangers in the world and applies the aggregated statistics to reach a more balanced and realistic figure picture of the currency market value.

Related words: exchangers

Bitminer

/ **bitminer** /

Noun

Noun: bitminer

1. Bitminer is a bitcoin mining pool which exist in forms of web-based applications, software-based application that uses the latest algorithms to mine, thereby enabling mining that allows for making as much money as possible.

Relate words: bit stamp, blockchain.

Bitmeter

/ bitmeter /
Adjective
Adjective: bitmeter
Definition

1. This is a bitcoin mining pool that aims to make it easy for anyone to make bitcoin.

Related words: asic, bitmain.

/ bit stamp /

Adjective
Adjective: bit stamp
Definition

1. This is a bitcoin exchange based in Luxembourg that allows trading between USD and Bitcoin.

2. Bitstamp allows for the usage of an exchange peer of USD to BTC.

Related words: bitmeter, etc.

Blocks
/ blaks /
Verb
Verb: blocks
Definition

1. A collection of transaction data gathered to a predetermined size and bundled up.

2. Blocks are bundled up transaction data, processed by investors for transaction verification

3. Transaction data is permanently recorded in files called blocks.

Related words: block chain, etc.

Blockchain

/ blockchain /
Adjective
Adjective: blockchain
Definition

1. The inter-linkage of several and differently created and processed blocks of currency transaction.
2. It is a publicly shared record of every bitcoin transaction that has ever being processed

Related words:

Block Reward

/ blak rəwɔrd /
Verb
Verb: block reward
Definition

1. A block reward or pay oof given to a miner who has successfully calculated the hash in a data block during a mining process

Related words: block reward

Block Time
/ blak tajm /
Adjective
Adjective: blocktime
Definitions

1. Block time refers to a new difficulty in BTC mining and BTC transactions which causes transactions to take an exhausting period of time before confirmation.

Related words:

Bollinger Bands
/ balɪŋər bændz /
Adjectives
Adjectives: Bollinger bands
Definitions

1. Bollinger Bands can be used to measure the "highness" or "lowness" of the price relative to previous trades.

2. Bollinger Bands are a volatility indicator

3. Bollinger Bands® are a highly

4. Popular technical analysis technique

Related words: Uptrend, Downtrend, Flat Trend

Bot Trading

/ bot tredɪŋ /
Verb
Verb: bot trading
Definitions

1. Bot trading refers to the usage of programs. tHe bots will trade automatically using the price criteria the investors have set.

Related words:

Breakaway Gap

/ brekəwe gæp /
Adjective
Adjective: breakaway gap
Definition

1. This represents a gap in the movement of stock prices which is supported and indicated by levels of high volume

Related words

Break Even
/ brek ivən /
Adjective:
Adjective: break even
Definition

1. This is a point in the cryptocurrency mining, where the individual or group of miners are neither making profits nor losses when cost of mining is calculated

Related words:

Broadcasting
/ brɔdkæstɪŋ /
Verb
Verb: broadcasting
Definition

1. This is the act of broadcasting the Hex of an unconfirmed transaction through a broadcast site so as to get transaction confirmation done

Related words: Hex

BTC
/btc /
Noun
Noun: BTC
Definition

1. This the first cryptocurrency by Satoshi Nakamoto

2. This is a digital payment system, digital currency, which uses harsh cash proof of work function for coin mining.

Acronym: bitcoin

Related words: dogecoin, litecoins etc

Bubble
/ bəbəl /
Adjectives
Adjectives: bubble
Definition

1. A bubble occurs when a stock in the market is driven upward by investors

Related words

Bull

/ bʊl/
Verb
Verb: bull
Defintition

1. A bull is an investor who thinks that a stock in the market or a security of some sort Is prone to a rise.

2. A bull is an individual who purchases security with the aim or an assumption of a rise and a profit when selling.

Related words: bullish, bearish, etc.

Bullish

/ˈbʊlɪʃ/
Adjectives
Adjectives; bullish
Definition

1. Bullishness is an act of buying security with the aim of selling at a profit after a market surge

2. Bullishness is a move towards investment based on an upsurge assumption in a market.

Related words: bull trap, bull, bull position

Bull Trap

/ bʊl træp /
Verb
Verb: bull trap
Definitions

1. A bull trap is the upward artificial drive of value by investors buying at large in order to fool traders into buying at inflated prices having the beliefs that the prices will continue to surge.

2. A false signal indicating, that a declining trend of a stock has reversed and its heading upwards

Antonyms: bear trap
Related words

Buy Order

/ baj ɔrdər /
Verb
Verb: buy order
Definition

1. This refers to a situation where and investor approaches, exchange and wants to purchase cryptocurrency

2. A buy order is an instructor from an investor to a broker to buy or invest in a commodity at a certain price.

Related words: sell order

C

Candlestick

/ kǽndəlstɪk /
Noun
Noun: candlestick
Definition

1. A candlestick is an important way to track market behavior and possible future directions.
2. A candlestick provides powerful analysis as information from the market is revealed.
3. A candlestick is a style of financial chart used to describe price movements of a security, derivative or currency.
4. A candlestick is a chart that displays the high lows, opening and closing prices of security for a specific period. A candlestick tells investors whether the closing price is higher or lower than the opening price

Synonyms: real body

Related words:

Center of Gravity

/ sɛntər əv grǽvəti /
Adjective
Adjective: center of gravity
Definition

1. This is a point in the bitcoin chart which indicate a rapid drop in price of bitcoin which recovers almost immediately or within a short period of time to its initial highs

Related words: graphs

Centralized

/ sɛntrəlàjzd /
Adjectives
Adjectives: centralized
Definition

1. The process by which the process the activities of an organization, planning, and decision-making becomes centralized within a particular group

Related words

Chaikin Money Flow

/ tʃékɪn məni fló /
Adjective
Adjective: chaikin money flow
Definition

1. This is a technical analysis indicator used to measure money flow volume over a set period of time

Abbreviations: CMF

Related word

Chargebacks

/ chargebacks /
Verb
Verb: chargebacks
Definition

1. This refers to the reversal of a bitcoin transaction after its being done without the intervention of a third party.

Related words: escrow service

Charts
/ tʃárts /
Noun
Noun: charts
Definition

1. This is a graphical representation of date with the use of symbols

2. This is the use a form of tabular numeric data for the representation of information using a qualitative structure

Related words: bar chart, line chart etc.

Circulation Supply
/sərkjəlèʃən səpláj //
Verb
Verb: circulation supply
Definition

1. This refers to the amount of cryptocurreny that has being mined and in circulation.

Related words:

Cloud mining

/ kláwd májnɪŋ /
Verb
Verb: cloud mining
Definition

1. This is a process of digital currency mining, by utilizing a remote data center with shared processing power.

Related words

Codes

/ kódz /
Noun
Noun: codes
Definitions

1. Codes are rule or methods used to encrypt a message

Related words: encryption

Coin

/ kɔjn /

Noun

Noun: coin

1. A coin is a flat disc or piece of metal with an official stamp, used as money.

Related words: digital currency, bitcoin.

Collective Mining

/ kəlɛktɪv májnɪŋ /

Verb

Verb: collective mining

1. This a cloud mining process which includes the collaboration of several organizations and enterprise businesses in the purchase of high-end expensive mining power, who in turn leasing the access to third parties.

2. This is a worked out pattern that makes mining affordable to individual miners who are regarded as left out

3. It is the usage or access to predetermined amount of mining power through cloud computing with the hassle of buying or maintaining the processing power to mine.

Related words: solo mining

Commodity Channel Index

/ kəmádəti tʃǽnəl ɪndɛks /
Adjectives
Adjectives: CCI
Definition:

1. This is a tool used by traders in identifying cyclical trends in currencies and commodities

Abbreviation: CCI
Related words: oscillator

Confirmation

/ kànfərméʃən /
Verb
Verb: confirmations
Definitions

1. This is the successful process of a block of transaction information or the successful mining of a block of information.

2. It means your transaction was processed by bitcoin miners and added to a new block on the blockchain

Related words: validation.

Consensus Protocols

/ kənsɛnsəs prótəkàlz /
Verb
Verb: consensus protocols
Definitions:

1. It ensures that the next lock in a block chain is the one and only version of the truth
2. It also keeps powerful adversaries from derailing the system and successfully forcing the chain

Related words: consensus algorithm, proof of work etc.

Consortium Blockchains

/ kənsɔrʃiəm blockchains /

Adjective

Adjective: consortium blockchains

Definition:

1. Consortium block chain is a blockchain that provides the hybrid functionality of public blockchain and private blockchains.

2. This is a block chain that provides part benefits of private and public blockchains in one.

Abbreviations:

Related words: private blockchain, public blockchain etc.

Continuation Graph Pattern

/ kəntɪnjuéʃən græf pǽtərn /

Verbs

Verbs: continuation graph pattern

Definitions

1. These are graphed patterns that show fluctuations that go against the flow of the current trend only to continue in the same direction afterward

2. A continuation graph shows that investors have tested the current market trend and found it to be sound so it therefore continues.

Related words: graph pattern

3.

Contracts

/ kántrækts /
Adjective
Adjective: contract
Definition:

1. A method of using cyptocurrency to form
   agreement with people on a block chain

Related words

Core

/ kɔr /
Noun
Noun: core
Definitions

1. A Core is programm used to decide which
   block chain contains valid transactions.

Related words: bitcoin core

Correction

/ kərɛkʃən /

Verb

Verb: correction

1. This is a negative reverse movement of at least 10% in a stock, bond, commodity or index in order to adjust an overvaluation in a stock market

2. These are temporal price declines interrupting a market uptrend

Related words: overvaluation

CPU Mining

/ CPU májnɪŋ /

Verb

Verb: CPU mining

Definitions

1. This is the use of a computer c.p.u to perform proof of work mining for different forms of cryptocurrencies or virtual currencies

Related words: proof of work

Crowdsource

/ crowdsource /
Verb
Verb: crowdsource
Definitions

1. This refers to the donation of money through the use of cryptocurrency

2. This is a process of getting funds usually online, from a crowd of people or investors

3. This is a collective financial gathering of cryptocurrency holders or investors that come from the public and then used to complete a business-related task

Related words: crowd funding,

Crowd Funding

/ kráwd fəndɪŋ /

Verb

Verb: crowd funding

Definitions

1. It refers to donations of either liquid or cryptocurrencies for the purpose of supporting certain ideas through designated platforms.

2. Crowdfunding is the practice of funding a project or venture by raising monetary contributions from huge numbers of investors.

3. It is the use of small amounts of capital from a large number of people to form a business venture.

Example: the (ICO) initial coin offering is a form of crowd funding based on cryptocurrency tokens

Related words: crowdsourcing, alternative finance, ICO,

Cryptocurrency
/ˈkriptōˌkərənsē/
noun
Noun: **cryptocurrency**

Definitions
1. a digital currency in which encryption techniques are used to regulate the generation of units of currency and verify the transfer of funds, operating independently of a central bank.

2. A cryptocurrency is a financial tool that takes the form of long blocks of alphanumeric code, and this alternative currency is traded between investors and used as a form of payment for goods and services to merchants who accept it.

Related words: *Bitcoin and Altcoins"*

Cryptocurrency Index

/ˈkriptōˌkərənsē/

Verb

Verb: cryptocurency index

Definitions
1. This is a benchmark for a crypto market dedicated to providing insight into the current and past movement of the market.

2. This is a conceptual measurement that uses algorithms to take into account that the cryptocurrency market is frequently changing

Abbreviation: *CRIX*

Related words: cryptographic protocol

Cryptography

/ krɪpˈtɒɡrəfi/
Verb
Verb: cryptography
Definitions

1. Cryptography is the science, study or the techniques of secret writing, especially codes

2. cryptography is most often associated with the process of scrambling clear text,

3. The science of coding and decoding messages so as to keep these messages secure,

Related words: coding

Cut and Handle Pattern

/kət ænd hændəl pætərn/

Noun

Noun: cut and handle pattern

Definition

1. This is 'u' shaped pattern on a chart with a light downward drift in the form a handle that forms a cup-like look on a chart.

2. Refers to a situation or pattern that happens when investors want to test the validity of an upward or a bullish trend in a commodity market.

Related words: charts, graphs, etc.

D

Darknet Markets

/darknet markəts/
Noun
Noun: darknet market
Definition:

1. This is a commercial website on the internet that operates via darknets like i2p or Tor

2. Darknet websites are black market websites that function primarily for the purpose of selling or brokering transactions involving drugs, weapons, stolen credit cards, counterfeit currencies etc.

Related words: crypto market,

Dash

/dæʃ/
Noun
Noun: dash
Definitions:

1. Open source peer to peer crypto currency used for instant online transactions

Related words: cryptocurrency, dark coin, x coin

Database

/detəbes/
Noun
Noun: database
Definitions:

1. This is a collection and organization of information so that it can be easily managed used and accessed.

2. A data is an organized structure of information that stored and accessed with computers

Related words: SQL server, database management system.

Day Trading

/de tredɪŋ /
Verb
Verb: DAY TRADING
Definitions:

1. This refers to daily trading of cryptocurrencies

2. Day trading is the act of keeping a close eye on one's investments, doing daily trades and keeping track of gains and losses by one's self or through the use of bot trading.

Related words: long term trading,

Dead Cat Bounce
/dɛd kæt bawns/
Verb
Verb: dead cat bounce
Definitions

1. A temporary recovery in long-term decline from a bear market.

2. A slight rebound from a prolonged downfall in the price of a stock

3. A brutal bearish trend

4. A sharp but short recovery from a substantial downfall in the price of any stock.

Related word: bearish trend,

Debt Registries

/dɛt rɛdʒəstriz/

Noun

Noun: debt registries

Definition

1. Debt registries help debtors check to know the legitimacy status of the debt collectors

2. A debt warehouse used in collecting information about debtors, debt collectors, and uncompleted debts

Related words: debt collector

Decentralized

/dəsɛntrəlajzd/

Adjective

Adjective: decentralized

Definitions

1. This means that cryptocurrencies are not issued or controlled by a central authority

2. This means that cryptocurrency is not affected by the regulations of any given government

3. It means the well being of a crypto currency's is dependent on the capabilities of the investors of a that currency

Related words: centralized

Deflation

/dəfleʃən /

Verb

Verb: deflation

Definition

1. This is the falling prices of market commodities, stocks, cryptocurrency and other investments.

2. A sharp or slow decrement in the price of marketable commodities

Related words: underwater.

Demurrage

/demurrage/
Adjective
Adjective: demurrage
Definition

1. This is a levied charged on long-term investors who keep coins for long-term gains

2. It is a way to prevent currency hoarding by charging levies on long-term investments.

Related words:

Deposit

/dəpazət/
Verb
Verb: deposit
Definitions

1. A sum of money paid into a financial institution

2. A sum of money paid or payable as a first installment on the purchase or as a pledge for a transaction.

Related words: cash

Depth Chart
/dɛpθ tʃart/
Adjective
Adjective: depth chart
Definition:

1. A market chart that shows the market's ability to sustain relatively large market activities without affecting the price of the security
2. A chart showing a market's ability to absorb buy and sell orders.

Related words: market depth, depth

Descending Triangle
/dəsɛndɪŋ trajæŋgəl/
Adjective
Adjective: descending triangle
Definition

1. This is a bearish chart pattern that in technical analysis that is created by drawing one trendline that connects a series of lower high and a higher high.

2. This is a chart that shows that the demand for an asset is weakening.

Related words: ascending triangle, bearish

Difficulty (Mining Difficulty)
/dɪfɪkəlti/
Adjective
Adjective: difficulty
Definition

1. This refers to the prolonged process of successfully mining data block information
2. It refers to the mining difficulty for a coin in relation to the specified algorithm

Related word: mining difficulty

Digital Currency
/dɪdʒətəl kərənsi/
Adjective
Adjective: digital currency
Definition

1. Digital currency is an electronic money which allows for instantaneous transaction and borderless transfer of ownership

Related words: digital money, electronic currency, vrtual currency etc.

Distributed Denial of Service (DDoS)
/dɪstrɪbjətəd dənajəl əv sərvəs/
Adjective
Adjective: distributed denial of service
Definitions

1. A DDoS attack is a form of cyber-attack targeted at computer networks in order to gain access to delicate information
2. DDoS are network attacks often designed to crash network servers

Related words: Warm, Trojan horse etc.

Dogecoin
/dogecoin/
Noun
Noun: Dogecoin
Definition

1. Decentralized online peer to peer currency or an electronic currency that enables people to easily send money online.

Related words: cryptocurrency, bitcoins, litecoins.

Double Bottom Pattern
/dəbəl batəm pætərn/
Adjective
Adjective: double bottom pattern

Definitions

1. A reversal pattered transitioning from a bear market to a bull market.

Related words: double top pattern

Double Spending
/ dəbəl spɛndɪŋ/
Verb
Verb: double spending
Definition

Double spending is a malicious attempt to pay for different services by two different people at the same time using the same bitcoin.

Related words: hackers.

Double Top Pattern
/dəbəl tap pætərn /
Adjective
Adjective: double top pattern
Definition

1. This is a reversal pattern on a market graph, indicating a transformation from a bull to a bear market.
2. A bearish trend or a downward trend on a market chart that happens as a result of a continuous buying and selling process in a market

Related words: double top pattern

Downtrend
/dawntrɛnd/
Adjective
Adjective: downtrend
Definitions

1. This describes the movement of a price in movement of a financial asset when the overall direction is downtrend

1) A successful peak which is lower than the one found in the earlier trend

Related words: uptrend

Dumping

/dəmpɪŋ/
Verb
Verb: jumping

Definitions

1. A predictor pricing in the context of international and cryptocurrency trade which is below cost prices.

2. A drastic fall in the price of commodities which comes as a result of massive sell out of coins

Related words: pricing, pumping

E

EH/S

/ɛ/ ɛs/

Adjective

Adjectives: EH/s

Definitions

1. This means exa hash per second;
2. This refers to the rate in which a computer completes an operation at exa hash rate billions

Related words: Hash Rate, Peta Hash, Giga Hash Etc.

Ehler Fisher Transform indicator

/ɛlər fɪʃər/

Adjectives

Adjectives: ehler fisher transform indicator

Definitions

1. A hidden dictator designed to find or spot major price reversals and visualize with a distinct and sharp turning point which shows spots where the rate of change is the biggest.

2. This is a financial chat used to transform shares prices following any probability distribution function into Gaussian normal distribution.

Related words:

Elder Force Index

/ɛldər fɔrs ɪndɛks/

Adjective

Adjective: elder force index

Definitions

1. This index, uses volumes and prices change from the previous close to determine the momentum behind a price move in a specific direction

Abbreviations: EFI.

Related words:

Elder Ray

/ɛldər re /

Adjective

Adjective: Elder Ray

Definitions

1. This is a technical indicator which is used to measure the amount of buying and selling pressure in a market

Abbreviations: ER

Related words: EMA

Electronic Money

/əlɛktranɪk məni/

Adjective

Adjective: electronic money

Definitions:

1. It is a monetary value that is stored electronically, used to make online payment transactions

2. Money which exists in computer banking systems and it's not held in any physical form.

3. Money exchanged electronically.

Abbreviation: e-money

Related words: digital currency, cryptocurrency, etc.

Encrypt
/ɛnkrɪpt/
Verb
Verb: decrypt
Definitions

1. Securing data by presenting such data or information in codes in order to prevent unauthorized access
2. The act of concealing information by converting such information into codes which may require extensive decryption processes.
3. This is the process of encoding data so that it becomes only accessible to authorized people only.

Related words: decrypt, codes, data.

Escrow

/ɛskro/
Verb
Verb: escrow
Definitions

1. This refers to a situation where a third party takes custody of the funds meant for a transaction until the transaction is approved and acknowledged by the chief parties
2. It is an account adopted by digital currencies for the purpose of trading large transactions, in order to give room for further investigations

Related words:

Etherum

/etherum/
Noun
Noun: eutherum
Definitions

1. Etherum is an open source, block chain base distributed computing platform featuring smart contract functionality which facilitates online contractual agreement

Related words: etherum classic,

Exchange

/ɪkstʃendʒ /
Verb
Verb: exchange
Definitions

1. An exchange is a cryptocurrency market base, where buyers and sellers are usually able to meet, in order do transactions.

2. A secure third party location were cryptocurrency traders either meet directly to transact or where the third parties buy from sellers and sell to other interested buyers. Thereby serving as middlemen

Related words:

Exchange Rate

/ɪkstʃendʒ ret/
Adjective
Adjective: exchange rate
Definitions:

1. This means how a cryptocurrency compares to other cryptocurrencies.
2. It also refers to how a currency stacks up against other currencies which could be liquid currency or digital currency

Related words: market rate,

Exchangers

/ɪkstʃendʒərz/
Adjective
Adjective: exchangers
Definitions

1. Individuals or organizations who use either online means or transact physically to buy cryptocurrency or liquid currency at rates below regular rates for the purpose of making a profit.

Related words: Digital currency exchanger, exchange etc.

Exhaustion Gap

/ɪgzɔstʃən gæp/
Adjective
Adjective: exhaustion gap
Definitions

1. This is a gap displayed on a graph which indicates a fall after a rapid rise in a stock price.
2. A gap that comes up at the end of an impulsive move
3. Gaps that happen close to a good up or down trend

4. This reflects a falling demand for a particular stock

Related words: breakaway gaps, run away gaps

Exponential Moving Average

/ɛksponɛntʃəl muvɪŋ ævərɪdʒ/

Adjective

Adjective: exponential moving average

Definitions:

1. This is a type of moving average that is similar to simple moving averages, that gives more weight to the most recent data

2. This is a signal of long-term trends

Related words: Moving average, simple moving averages. Exponential weighted moving average

F

F.O.M.O

/ɛf o ɛm o/

Adjective

Adjective: fear of missing out

Definition:

1. This is a feeling you get when a certain coin is being pumped up like crazy with two- digit gains in few minutes

Acronym: Fear Of Missing Out

Related words:

F.U.D

/ɛf ju di/

Verb

Verb: F.U.D

Definitions:

1. An activity is done to put people at a disadvantage
2. An act masterminded by companies to put people in an appalling position

Acronyms: Fear, Uncertainty, And Doubt

Related words:

Falling Wedge

/falıŋ wɛdʒ/
Adjective
Adjective: falling wedge
Definition

1. This is a bullish trend that begins wide at the top and contracts as prices on the chart moves lower.

Related words: bullish

Faucet

/fɔsət /
Noun
Noun: faucet
Definition

1. Faucets are ordained programs designed to offer cryptocurrencies to people at a free
2. Web sites that offer free cryptocurrency to attract attention

Related words: websites

Fiat Currency

/fajæt kərənsi/

Definitions:

1. A financial tool that is not backed up by any physical commodity,

2. All kinds of currencies, both physical and digital that can be used for transactions are fiat currencies

Related words: physical currency, digital currency

Fill or Kill

/fɪl ɔr kɪl /

Verb

Verb: fill or kill

Definitions

1. This refers to the fulfilling of investors demand a number of coins needed at specific prices before specified deadlines

2. Filling up transaction request within a specified period of time or putting that transaction to an end.

Related words: transactions

Flag Pattern

/flæg pætərn/
Adjective
Adjective: flag pattern
Definitions

1. A one to three weeks uncertain pattern of a market trend displayed on a chart, which appears to be bullish and bearish, caused by a test in the trend of a commodities value.

Related words: chart, bearish, bullish etc.

Fork

/fɔrk/
Verb
Verb: fork

Definition

1. Fork happens when two miners find a valid hash within a short space of time

Related words: Accidental Fork, Hard Fork, Gift Fork

Fontas

/fontas/
Noun
Noun: fontas

Definition

1. Unidentifiable investors who use schemes called dump and bump to manipulate the value of a currency in the market.

2. Individuals who buy large chunks of coins at a low price and then use misleading information to get investors to buy at a higher price.

Related words: dump and bump, etc.

FPGA Mining

/FPGA majnɪŋ/
verb
verb: FPGA mining

Definitions

1. This refers to the use of a FPGA hardware as a mining tool

2. The use of FPGA board for mining either on a mining pool or for solo mining

Related words: Bitcoin mining, hardware mining

Fractal Chaos Bands
/fræktəl keas bændz/
Adjectives
Adjectives: fractal chaos bands
Definition:

1. This is a chart indicator, that reflects the trend lines of a market by indicating two lines that are plotted through the highest and the lowest values of the market on a specific time period.

Abbreviations: FCB

Related words: fractal chaos oscillator

Fractal Chaos Oscillator
/fræktəl keas asəletər/

Adjective
Adjective: fractal chaos oscillator
Definitions:

1. This is a chart indicator, which goes back in time depending on the chosen time to check the choppiness versus it trendiness and expresses it in numeric value

Abbreviations: FCO
Related words: fractal chaos bands

Full Node

/ fʊl nod/

Adjective

Adjective: full node

Definition

1. A full node is a computer that connects to a computer network and operates under all the rules of Bitcoin

2. A full node is a node that downloads every block of a transaction and checks them against bitcoin core consensus rules.

Related words: lightweight nodes, nodes, etc.

Fundamental Analysis

/fəndəmɛntəl ənæləsəs/
Adjective
Adjectives: Fundamental

Definition

1. This is a method of evaluating a security or an investment in an attempt to secure its value.

2. This is an analysis that provides a comprehensive information on anything that can affect the value of a security or investment.

Related words:

G

Genesis Block

/dʒɛnəsəs blak /
Adjective
Adjective: genesis block

Definition

1. The first block of data mined in order to lunch of a digital currency.

2. An initial block on the chain which its initial hashes set to all zeros, signifying the first stages of a new coin mining process

Related word: block chain, coin, and mining. Etc.

Genesis Mining

/dʒɛnəsəs majnɪŋ/
Verb
Verb: genesis mining
Definitions
1. This is the largest cloud mining company on the internet

2. This is the world's leading and most transparent hosting hash power service provider for investors who intend to mine cryptocurrencies

Related words: mining

GH/S

/ gh εs/
Adjective
Adjective: GH/s
Definitions

1. This refers to the rate in which a computer or a cryptocurrency miner is generating, in hashes per seconds

2. The refers to the capabilities of a mining tool

Acronyms: Giga Hash
Related words:

GPU Hardware

/GPU hardwεr/
Adjective
Adjective: gpu hardware

Definition

1. A GPU graphic card which runs ETHASH algorithm key which is used as a key to the proof of work in ethereum

Acronym: Graphics processing unit
Related words:

Graphs Gaps

/græfs gæps/
Adjectives
Adjectives: graph gaps

Definitions:
  a. A visible drop or rise in the value of a commodity which happens as a result of closed markets or statistical adjustments identified by a market value graph

Related words: breakaway gaps, runaway gap, exhaustion gap, etc.

H

Hackers

/hækərz/

Noun

Noun: hacker

Definition:

1. This refers to a skilled computer expert that uses such skills to a bug or exploit computer systems and networks.

Related words: DDoS, Programmers, Computing

Hard Fork

/hard fɔrk/

Adjective

Adjective: hard fork

Definitions:

1. This is a form blockchain technology which is used to make valid previous blocks/transaction which is invalid or vice versa.
2. A radical change in blockchain technology where blocks and transactions are reversed from previous states of validity or invalidity

Related words: etherum

Hardware

/hardwɛr/

Noun

Noun: hardware

Definition

1. A physical component that constitutes any computing technology.

2. The physical parts of a computer system.

Related words: computer, technology

Hardware Mining

/hardwɛr majnɪŋ /

Verb

Verb: hardware mining

Definition

1. This refers to customized equipment used that pushes the performance of mining higher
2. The use of field programmable gateway array processor that use much less power to create a concentrated mining farm

Related words FPGA

Hash

/hæʃ/
Adjective
Adjective: hash
Definition

1. This refers to taking an input in return for a fixed size alphanumeric string which is called hashing

2. This is a systematic scientific algorithm used to create checksu
3. This is used to identify the authenticity of a piece of data

Related words: cryptographic hashing

Hash Power

/hæʃ pawər/
Adjective
Adjective: hash power
Definition

1. This is an innovative cloud mining system

2. This is an asset management service at the cryptocurrency market, which includes developing mining processed of bitcoin

Related words: cloud mining.

Hash Rate

/hæʃ ret/

Adjectives

Adjectives: hash rate

Definition:

1. This refers to the speed at which mathematical calculations are done, while mining data blocks of digital currencies

2. Hash rates are measurement criteria's used to determine the speed at which a crypto currency can be mined and the quantity of currency expected from each mining activity.

Related words: kilo hashes, mega hashes giga hashes, peta hashes

Head and Shoulders Pattern

/hɛd ænd ʃoldərz pætərn/

Adjectives

Adjectives: heads and shoulder pattern

Definition

1. A market value chart pattern here two smaller chart fluctuations in value happen to bracket a larger one in the middle.

Related words: traditional heads and shoulders, regular heads and shoulders etc.

Hodl

/hodl/

Adjective

Adjective: hodl

Definition

1. This is an enthusiastic misspelling of the word 'hold' ;
2. This a word used in prompting investors not to sell their coins and 'hold' when prices are on the high

Related words: Holding.

Hybrid Wallet

/hajbrəd wɔlət /

Adjective

Adjective: hardware wallet

Definition:

1. This is a combination of a software wallet and a web wallet meant for storage and maintenance of cryptocurrency which is stored on a third parties host server.

Related words: Private key.

Hyperledger

/hyperledger/
Adjective
Adjective: hyperledger
Definitions

1. This is a global collaboration, created to advice cross-industry blockchain

2. This is a project of open source blockchain and related tools to support the collaborative development of blockchain based ledgers

Related words: Linux Foundation, blockchain, distributed ledgers

I

I.C.O/I.T.O.

/aj si o/ aj ti o /
Verb
Verb: I.C.O/ I.T.O

1. The I.C.O is an unregulated means by which funds are raised for a new cryptocurrency venture.

Related words:

I.O.U

/aj o ju/
Noun
Noun: IOU
Definitions

1. I.o.u is a document that indicates that a debt which may not necessarily involve monetary value exists.

Acronyms: I owe you
Related words: loan notes

I.P.O

/aj pi o/
Adjective
Adjective: I.P.O
Definitions:

1. This refers to the first time a stock is offered to the general public by a company seeking capital to expand or for public trading

Abbreviations: Initial Public Offerings, Going Public
Related words:

Indicators

/ ɪndəketərz/
Adjective
Adjective: indicators
Definitions:

1. This is the statistic used by investors to measure and to forecast current economic and financial trend.

Related words: technical indicators

Inflation

/ɪnfleʃən/

Verb

Verb: Inflation

Definition

1. The term inflation refers to the act of buying commodities at a low price and waiting a prolonged period of time when the value of such assets must have risen before selling at high prices.

Related words: Deflation, Pricing etc.

Insta-mine

/insta majn/

Definitions:

1. This is the distribution of coins in an unfair manner
2. This is the issuance of a large supply of all future available coins during a few hours on the lunch day

Related words: initial coin distribution

Intraday Momentum Index
/ ɪntrəde momɛntəm ɪndɛks/
Adjectives
Adjectives: intraday momentum index
Definition

1. This is a technical indicator that combines the relative strength index with candlestick analysis in order to provide investors with potential buying and selling days based off of signals created on individual days.

Abbreviations: I. M .I
Related words:

Investing/Investments
/ɪnvɛstɪŋ ɪnvɛstmənts/
Verb
Verb: investing
Definition

1. The allocation of finance or property in the expectation of future benefits or asset acquisition

Related words: Arbitrage, Investor

Investors

/ɪnvɛstərz /

Noun
Noun: investors
Definition

1. This refers to an individual who commits capital for the purpose financial returns
2. Anyone involved in either high or low-risk investment with the aims of making profit

Related words: Investments

Issuer

/ɪʃuər/
Noun
Noun: issuer
Definition:

1. This is a concept used in a type of cryptocurrency to refer to its investors.

Related words: Investors, Decentralized,

J

JOMO

Adjective
Adjective: JOMO
Definition

1. This is regarded as a response to FOMO

2. This refares to the joy of missing out on a bearish turn out in a market trend or on investment Accronyms: joy of missing out

Related words: FOMO

KH/S
/kh ɛs/
Adjective
Adjective:KH/s
Definitions

1. This refers to a cryptocurrency mining hash power which in thousands of hashes per second
2. This is the rate at which a dedicated miner, CPU or graphics card can mine blocks of data

Related words: MG/s, GG/s etc.

Keltner Channel
/kɛltnər tʃænəl/
Adjective
Adjective: Keltner channel
Definitions

1. A volatility-based indicator which is used to measure the rate of stock in relation to an upper or lower moving average band

Related words: trading band, turtle channel etc.

Key

/ ki/

Noun

Noun: key

Definition

1. This is a piece of data that determines the functional output of a cryptographic algorithm

2. This is a piece that specifies the transformation of clear text in cipher text

Related words: codes, algorithm, encryption etc.

L

Ledger
/lɛdʒər/

Adjective
Adjective: ledger
Definition

1. This is a book or file which is used to for keeping records and totaling economic transactions measured in financial terms of a monetary unit of account.

Related words: bookkeeping, debit, and credit e.t.c

Level Wedge
/lɛvəl wɛdʒ/

Adjective
Adjective: level wedge
Definition

1. This pattern represents a brief respite from the trend preceding it and once it's formed, the trend will continue in that direction

Related words: Wedge pattern, market graphs

Leverage Trading

/lɛvərɪdʒ tredɪŋ /
Adjective
Adjective: leverage trading
Definition

1. This is the ability to trade larger amounts with small capitals

2. This is the ability for an investor to trade almost the 20:1, 50:1, which is far more than initial capital.

Related words: investors, markets e.t.c

Linear Reg Forecast

/lɪniər rɛg fɔrkæst/
Adjective
Adjective: linear reg forecast
Definition

1. Forecasting approach;

2. This is a methods of modeling a scalar department between a scalar dependent and an explanatory variable

Related words: multivariate linear regression

Linear Reg R2

/lɪniər rɛg r2/

Agjective

Adjective

Definition:

1. It measures the percent of variation in a y variable which can be attributed to variation in the x variable

Litecoin

/lite coin/

Noun

Noun: lite coins

Definitions

1. This is a form of digital currency which uses the proof of work method for its mining, and a script mining algorithm.

Related words: bitcoins, dogecoin, digital currency.

Long-term Trading

/lɔŋ tərm tredɪŋ/
Verb
Verb: long-term trading
Definitions:

1. This is the act of making fewer transactions that make larger individual gains
2. This is referred to the act of taking a position that reflects a long-term prediction.

Related words: day-to-day-trading

Lower Shadow

/loər ʃædo /
Adjective
Adjective: lower shadow
Definition

1. This is regarded as a weak bullish signal on a market chart that has significant when the market is oversold or at support.

Related words: candlestick

M

MH/S
/ɛmetʃ ɛs/
Adjective
Adjective: MH/s
Definition

1. This refers to term, mega hashes per seconds
2. This is the rate at which a mining tool can hash trough mathematical calculations and
3. This is called mining power in mega hashes

Related words: Giga hashes, peta hashes, tera hashes

M.L.M
/ ɛm ɛl ɛm/
Adjective
Adjective: M.L.M
Definition

1. This is a pyramid scaling network marketing used by companies to encourage their existing distributors by paying the existing distributors some incentives for their recruits

Acronyms; Minimum Level Marketing

Related words:

Market

/markət/
Noun
Noun: market
Definitions

1. This is a medium that allows buyer and sellers of different commodities to exchange services and goods for monetary gains.

Related words:

Market Cap

/markət kæp/
Adjective
Adjective: market cap
Definition

1. This is the market value of company's outstanding shares
2. Outstanding market stock evaluation

Acronym: market capitalization

Related words

Master node
/masternode/
Noun
Noun: masternode

Definition

1. This is the second tier of network in a dash coin's two-tier network which performs the functions of private send, instant send and governance function

Related words: coinjoin, instant send, private send etc.

Max Supply
/mæks səplaj /
Adjective
Adjective: max supply

Definition

1. This is a situation when certain cryptocurrencies have a maximum transfer rate allowed for a private send transaction e.g 1000 dash

Related words: litecoins, dash coins private send etc.

Miners

/majnərz/
Noun
Noun: miners

Definitions

1. Individual or group of individuals who do the process of adding transaction records to a digital currency's public ledger of past transaction
2. This is also used to refer to a mining application used by a person to mine block off the digital currency.

Related words: mining, mining tool, solo mining. etc.

Mining

/majnɪŋ/
Verb
Verb: mining
Definitions

1. This is a process of making computers do complex mathematical calculations for a cryptocurrency network to confirm user bitcoin transactions in a block.

2. A process of generating new coins for certain cryptocurrencies

3. The process of seeking reward from being able to solve certain mathematical calculations

Relative words; calculative hashes

Mining Ecosystem
/majnɪŋ ikosɪstəm/

Adjective

Adective: mining eco system

Definition

1. A comparison page where specifications and performances details of mining hardware are carefully logged for reference.

Related words: mining

Mining Pools
/majnɪŋ pulz/
Adjective
Adjective: mining pool

1. A mining process which involves more than one miner
2. A group of miners who put their resources together to ensure that mining is easier and more successful as individual mining is expensive

Related words: mining,

Mintage Cap

/mɪntədʒ kæp/

Adjective

Adjective: mintage cap

Definition

1. Mintage cap refers to the number of coins that can be mined before a cryptocurrency reaches its final cap or limitation where no more coins can be mined.

Related words: mining

Mobile Wallet

/mobəl wɔlət/
Adjective
Adjective: mobile wallet

Definition

1. This is a way to carrying information of a
   financial tool in a digital form on a mobile
   device.

2. This is a form of software wallet which is
   used to store private keys and do hot/cold
   functions for their carriers

3. This is an application available on a
   mobile device e.g Jaxx wallet, mycelium
   e.t.c

Related words: paper wallet, hardware wallet,
e.t.c

Momentum Indicator
/momɛntəm ɪndəketər/
Noun
Noun: momentum indicator
Definition

1. A momentum idicator compares the prices is in relation to where the same price was in the past.
2. This is a chart indicator that compares similar price in different time frames

Related words:

Monero
/monero/
Noun
Noun: monero
Definition

1. This is an open source crypto currency which is focused basically on privacy, decentralization, and scalability

2. This is a digital currency based on the crypto note protocol and poses significant algorithmic differences that relate to blockchain obfuscation

Related words: bitcoin, dogecoin e.t.c.

Money Flow Index

/məni flo ındɛks/

Adjective

Adjective: money flow index

Definition

1. This is a form of oscillator that uses both prices and volume to measure to measure buying and selling pressure.

Abbreviation: MFI

Related words; oscillator

Moving Average

/muvıŋ ævərıdʒ /

Adjective

Adjective: moving average

Definition

1. This is a technical analysis indicator that helps to smooth out price action by filtering out the noise from the from the random price fluctuations

Abbreviations: MA

Related words: simple moving average, exponential moving average.

Moving Average Convergence

/muvɪŋ ævərɪdʒ kənvərdʒəns/

Adjective

Adjective: moving average convergence

Definition

1. A trading indicator used in analysis stock market prices by revealing the changes in strength, direction, momentum, and duration of a trend in a stock's price.

Related words: exponential movng aerage

Divergence

/dajvərdʒəns/

Definition:

1. This is a trading indicator used in technical analysis of a stock price

2. This is a sort of trend-following momentum indicator that shows the relationship between several moving averages of prices

Abbreviations: MACD

Related Words: Exponential Moving Averages

Moving Average Envelope

/muvɪŋ ævərɪdʒ ɛnvəlop /
Definition

1. This is a type of technical indicator that is formed by two moving averages that define upper and lower price range levels

Abbreviations: MAE
Related words: moving averages

Multi-signature Wallets

/məlti sɪgnətʃər wɔləts/
Definition
1. A digital signature scheme that allows for numerous users to sign a single document

Abbreviation: MSW

Related words: software wallet, hardware wallet etc.

N

Network

/nɛtwərk/

Noun

Noun: network

Definition

1. A network is used to support Bitcoin transactions as simple broadcast network using TCP to propagate transactions and blocks

2. A network is a set of networked computer devices using transfer protocols to send data across nodes

Related words: dos, ddos, computers,nodes e.t.c

Ninja Launch

/nɪndʒə lɔntʃ/

Verb

Verb: ninja lunch

Definition:

1. This refers to the lunch of a ninja cloud mining system with an admin interface that allows users to lease reasonably priced mining hardware

Related words ninjacolo

Noob

/noob/
Adjective
Adjective: noob
Definitions

1. A new comer to the world of cryptocurrency
2. Individuals or new investors who have little knowledge about specific market trends and how cryptocurrency works

Related words: new blood, newb,

Novacoin

/nova coin/
Noun
Noun: nova coin
Definitions

1. This is a type of digital currency which uses script mining algorithm and is mined by the combination of proof of work and proof of stake methods

Related words: lite coin, dodge coin, eutherum classic, etc.

Offline Storage
/offline stɔrədʒ/
Adjective
Adjective: offline storage
Definitions

1. The act of keeping digital currency off internet access

2. A safety mechanism introduced alongside digital currency which makes sure an investment or possession isn't connected directly to one person or accessible over the internet

Related words: online storage

Oscillator
//
Noun
Noun: oscillator
Definition

1. This is a technical analysis tool banded between two extreme values and it is built with a result of short-term overbought or oversold conditions

Related words: stochastic oscillator

On Balance Volume
/an bæləns valjum/

Adjective
Adjective: on balance volume
Definition:

1. This is a momentum indicator that required the usage of volume flow to predicts the change in a stock price

Related words: smart money
Abbreviations: OBV

Open Source
/opən sɔrs /
Adjective
Adjectives: opensource
Definition

1. This refers to any program with a source code, made available for general usage and modification as users or other developers see fit.

2. Opensource program is freely available to the general public.

Abbreviation: OSS
Related words: Linux, shared sources, free software.

Open ledger
/ opən lɛdʒər/

Adjectives
Adjectives: open ledger
Definitions

I.   This offer third parties the opportunity to
     hold an amount on a specific account
     short term for further use for funds,
     providing a legal hub for investors

Related words:

Oracles
/ ɔrəkəl/

Noun
Noun: oracles
Definitions

1. An oracle is any system which provides
   extra information on a system which is not
   generally available.
2. A system which responds to every query
   with a random response gotten from its
   output domain.

Related words: software development kit.

Order

/ɔrdər/

Adjective
Adjective: order
Definition

1. This refers to customers electronic instructions issued through the site which for matching, which may be a buy or a sell instruction.
2. It is the arrangement of customer instruction to sell or buy in sequence

Related words: order book, crypto next

Order Book

/ɔrdər bʊk/
Adjective
Adjective: order book
Definition

1. This is an order book is a ledger containing all outstanding instructions from trader to buy or sell type of crypto currency
2. This is an order book of sequential arrangement of sell and buy instructions

Related words: sell order, buy order, market order limit order

P

PH/S
/pietʃ ɛs/
Adjective
Adjective:ph/s
Definition

1. This means peta hashes per second

2. This refers to the hash power of a mining tool at which is at one quadrillion hashes per second

Related words: Gh/S, Th/S, harsh rate, etc.

Paper Trade
/pepər tred/
Adjective
Adjective: paper trade
Definition

1. This is a trading process in which the investors can learn trading without using real currency.
2. This is a simulated trading process through which an individual can practice trading without the use of real money

Related words: virtual stock trading

Paper Wallet

/pepər wɔlət/
Adjective
Adjective: paper wallet
Definition

1. This is a document that contains all the data necessary for generating any number of bitcoin private keys
2. A way of storing bitcoin as a physical document

Related words: wallets, web-based key generator.

Parabolic SAR

/pɛrəbalık sar/
Adjective
Adjective: Parabolic SAR
Definition

1. This is an indicator that is mainly used by a trader to determine the future short term momentum of an asset.
2. This is a complex indicator that enables a trader to determine where a stop order should be placed during a trading process.

Related words: parabolic indicator, stock appreciation right.

Pass-Through

/pæs θru/
Adjective
Adjective: pass- through
Definitions

1. This is a pool of fixed income securities that is backed by a package of assets.
2. This is the rate on an access pool with security

Related words: fixed income security.

Peer-to-Peer

/pɪr tu pɪr/
Adjective
Adjective: peer to peer
Definitions

1. a situation where transactions are made between merchant and investors or vice versa without any centralized authority

Related words: decentralized

Peercoin
/peercoin/
Noun
Noun: peercoin
Definition:

1. This is known as peer-to-peer coin or digital currency which uses SHA-256 as a mining algorithm and is mined by a combination of proof of work and proof of stake method

Related words: cryptocurrency, bitcoin, altcoins, etc.

Pending Transaction
/pɛndɪŋ trænzækʃən/
Adjective
Adjective: pending transaction
Definition

1. This is transactions such as cash deposits, direct deposits, a point of sale purchases, cryptocurrency, and transfer of funds that are already submitted but is yet to clear your account.

Related words: confirmed transaction.

Pennant Pattern

/pɛnənt pætərn/
Adjective
Adjective: pennant pattern
Definition:

1. This is a pennant shape formed on a market value chart pattern when investors want to test a current trend in a commodity value.

Related words: bear, bull

Platform Exchange

/plætfɔrm ɪkstʃendʒ/
Adjective
Adjective platform exchange
Definitions:

1. This is a digital currency exchange that limits transaction facilitation but creates a secure platform for transactions between investors only.

Related words: Exchange, exchangers.

PoD (Proof of Developer)

/pruf əv dɪvɛləpər/
Adjective
Adjectives: PoD
Definition:

1. This is a program done in order to bring the crypto community closer, with trusted/trustworthy developers,
2. This is a program designed as well to give investors surety as the program remedies the scam coins by doing an analysis of the coins developers.

Related words: coin developers, crypto Asian.

Positions

/pəzɪʃənz/
Adjectives
Adjectives: positons
Definitions:

1. This refers to when funds are borrowed and a trade is opened for buying and selling.

Related words: long position, short position.
Open positions, short positions.

Power Cost
/pawər kast/
Adjective
Adjectives: power cost
Definitions

1. This refers to the cost or the amount of money to be spent on providing power supply for your mining process in order to prevent system outage and system crash

Related words: avoiding downtime, power up

Power Watts (used)
/pawər wats/
Adjective
Adjective: power watts
Definitions:

1. Power consumption of an electrical component used in mining
2. This is the measurement of the amount of power consumed by an electrical component.

Related words: watt formula, electrical power

Pre mine
/pri majn/
Verb
Verb: per mine
Definitions:

1. This is an altcoin that defies the regular mining and distribution convention
2. This is an altcoin that is exclusively redistributed by its users while block rewards are generated by transaction fees only.
3. This is also where a developer keeps a certain amount of coins credit to a particular address before exposing its source code.

Related words: instamine, etc.

Price Index
/prajs ındɛks/
Adjective
Adjective: price index
Definitions:

1. This is a normalized average of price relatives for a given class of services in certain locations at certain periods of time.

2. A percentage number that shows the rate at which a price has changed over a period of time.

Abbreviation: PI
Related words: customer price index

Price Volume Trend

/prajs valjum trɛnd/
Adjectives
Adjective: price volume index
Definition

1. A trend indicator consisting of a cumulative volume line that adds or deducts a multiple of the percentage change in share prices trend and present volume, depending on the upward or downward movement

2. A variation of on balance volume.

Abbreviation: PVT
Related words: technical analysis tool.

Private Blockchain

/prajvət blockchain/
Adjective
Adjective: private blockchain
Definition

1. This is a blockchain with an access control layer built into its protocol

2. A blockchain with a diverse level of security than a public blockchain.

Related words: public block chain, shared database.

165

Private Key

/prajvət ki/
Adjective
Adjective: private key
Definition

1. This is a unique identifier code that is used by digital currency investors in order to carry out a transaction.

2. This is a key that serves functions similar to credit cards as they used to access encrypted transaction.

Related word: public keys e.t.c

Proof-of-Stake

/pruf əv stek /
Adjective
Adjective: proof of stake
Definition

1. This is a form reward that comes with mining of amounts you have already invested. The more the currency held, the higher your potential reward for mining will be.

Related words: proof of work, investment

Proof-of-Work

/pruf əv wərk/
Adjective
Adjective: proof of work
Definition

1. Proof of work mining requires a computer processor to perform calculations called hashes

Related words: proof of stake

Public Blockchain

/pəblɪk blockchain/

1. This is a blockchain technology designed to cut off the need for middlemen in any asset or exchange scenario
2. This is an appropriate technology for decentralized networks

Abbreviations: PBC
Related words: private blockchain, consortium blockchain etc.

Public Key
/ pəblɪk ki/
Adjective
Adjectives: public key
Definitions

1. This is a form specially encrypted code issued to coin investors
2. This a set of code used for public transaction.
3. It serves as a public identifier for an investor when making transactions.

Related words: private keys.

Pump and Dump
/pəmp ænd dəmp/
Verb
Verb: pump and dump
Definitions:

1. This refers to a situation when investors buy coins cheaply and in very high quantity, publicize (pump) the coin, then do a heavy sell out of such coins to other investors, thereby (dumping) the price.

Related words: dump, pump

Pumping
/pəmpɪŋ/
Verb
Verb: pumping
Definitions:

1. This refers to the act of purchasing cryptocurrency at low value in very high quantity, thereby falsely causing an upward surge in demand due temporarily increased priced

Related words: dumping,

Q

QR code

/qr kod/

Noun

Noun: QR code

Definition:

1. A QR code is used in the crypto world to store information such as URLs, and private keys.

2. It is used by merchants who accept crypto currency to take payment from their customers

Related words: Bar code,

R

R.O.I

/ar o aj/
Adjective
Adjective: ROI

Definitions

1. This is the return of benefit from an investment which is relative to the cost of investment
2. The measure of the gains or losses generated by investments.

Abbreviations: Return on investment
Related words: net profit, cost of investment e.t.c

REKT

/rekt//
Noun
Noun: REKT

Definition

1. This is an internet slang which is shorthand for wrecked

2. It used for individual who lost basically all their investments from trading a certain digital currency or any other investment

Related words: stop loss

Real Body

/ ril badi/
Adjective
Adjective: real body

Definitions

1. This in candlestick is a representation of the range between open market prices and closed market prices

Related words shadows

Recovery Phrases

/rɪkəvri frezəz /

Noun

Noun: recovery phase

Definition

1. This is a phrased used to recover funds into an entirely new wallet, in cases of loss of devices like mobile phones

Related words: wallet words, backup phrase.

Referrals Commissions

/rəfərəlz kəmɪʃənz/

Adjective

Adjective : referral commission

Definition

1. This is a sort of commission an individual gets from referring people into an affiliate program
2. This are earning that comes in form of bonus from the trading activities of individual referrals

Related words: referrals

Relative Strength Index

/rɛlətɪv strɛŋkθ ɪndɛks/

Adjective

Adjective: relative strength index

Definition

1. This is a momentum oscillator that measures speed and the changes in movement of prices in the market

2. This is used to analyse a financial market by charting the current and historical strength of a market

Abbreviation: RSI

Related words: oscillator, technical indicator.

Remittance Network

/rimɪtəns nɛtwərk /
Adjective
Adjective: remittance network
Definition

1. This refers to the amount of money sent by an individual to his or her home country

2. This is a global free financial transaction system supported by ripple with no chargebacks using ripple transaction protocol

Abbreviation: RN
Related words: ripple, RTXP

Reversal Graph Pattern

/ rıvərsəl græf pætərn/

Noun

Noun: reversal graph pattern

Definition:

1. This is a market graph value chart which indicates that a bull trend may become a bear market or vice versal

2. This is a form of market graph value chart that is shown on numerous exchange websites.

Related words: bull market, bear market

Reverse Indicator

/rıvərs ındəketər/

Noun

Noun: reverse indicator

Definition

1. This is a method of acquiring lateral offset measurements of two shaft that are approximately causal
2. This is a technical analysis tool on a chart which indicates a reverse in the market value of a commodity

Related words: oscillator

Ripple

/ rɪpəl /
Noun
Noun: Ripple
Definition:

1. This is a distributed financial technology utilized by banks to send real-time international payments.

2. This is also a genuine digital currency or altcoin

Related words: XRP

Rising Wedge

/ rajzɪŋ wɛdʒ/
Adjectives
Adjective: rising wedge
Definition

1. This is a chart pattern wich is known to be bearish and is usually found in downtrends.
2. This is a chart pattern that develops when prices records higher tops and higher bottoms

Related words: falling wedge, chart pattern.

Rounding Bottom

/rawndɪŋ batəm /
Adjective
Adjective: rounding bottom
Definition:

1. A rounding bottom is a value chart on an exchange website which is considered as a reversal pattern.
2. A round bottom trend is a reversal pattern indication the transition from an upward trend to a downward trend or vice versa.

Related words: reversal graph indicator, saucer bottom

Runaway Gap

/rənəwe gæp/
Adjective
Adjective: runaway gap
Definition

1. This is a gap that happens in a strong bullish or bearish movement determined by a change in price and appearing over a change of prices.

Related words: breakaway gap.

Saj Candle

/saj kændəl/
Noun
Noun: saj candle
Definitions:

1. This is a price chart for saj.

Related words:

Satoshi

/satoʃi/
Noun
Noun: satoshi
Definition

1. Satoshi is smaller fractions of bitcoins.

2. It is the smallest possible fractions of cryptocurrencies.

Related words: Bitcoins, Altcoins, Satoshi Nakamoto.

Saucer Bottom

/sɔsər batəm/
Noun
Noun: saucer bottom
Definition:

1. This is a technical chart indicator that shows that the price of a commodity has reached its low and it's about to reverse

Related words:

Schaff Trend Cycle

/ ʃæf trɛnd sajkəl/
Noun
Noun: Schaff Trend Cycle
Definition

1. This is a technical analysis indicator which shows solid and overbought market conditions

Related words: moving averages.

Scrypt

/skrɪpt /
Adjective
Adjective: script

Definition

1. This is a type of mining algorithm used by cryptocurrencies because it is quicker and easier to use

2. This is a mining algorithm used by altcoins like lite coin and Nova coin as mining algorithms

Related words: SHA-256, mining.

Sell Order

/sɛl ɔrdər/
Verb
Verb: sell order

Definition

1. This is an investor's order or interest to sell out all his/her investments.

Related words: script

SegWit

/segwit/
Adjective
Adjective: segwit
Definition

1. This means segregated witness

2. This is a proposed solution to bitcoin scaling problem

3. This is a proposed update to bitcoin core, directed towards solving transaction malleability

Related words: Bitcoin core,

SHA 256
/ʃa 256/
Noun
Noun: sha 256
Definitions

1. This is a mining protocol which requires lots of CPU power and processing time.
2. It is a mining algorithm used by cryptocurrencies such as bitcoins and peercoin

Related words: script

Signing/Signature
/sajnɪŋ / sɪgnətʃər/
Verb
Verb: signing
Definition

1. This is a digital signature

2. This is a cryptographic Vue that is calculated from the data and secret key known only by the signer

3. This is a technique that binds a person to the digital data.

Related words: digital signature, encryption, pubic key, private key

Silk Road
/sɪlk rod/
Adjective
Adjective: silk road
Definition

1. This is an online platform designed for selling illegal things
2. This is a part of the dark web and the first modern darknet market

Related words: darknet, black market

Simple Moving Average
/sɪmpəl muvɪŋ ævərɪdʒ/
Adjective
Adjective: simple moving average
Definition:

1. This is an arithmetic moving average calculated by adding the closing prices of the security for a number of time periods and then dividing this total by the number of time periods

Abbreviations: SMA
Related words: moving average, closing prices etc.

SliceFeeds
/slice feeds/
Adjective
Adjective: slice feeds
definition
1. This is a new social platform for traders, investors, and enthusiasts
2. This is a resource for digital currency traders. the major aim is in informing and educating crypto investors

Related words: slices

Slices
/slajsəz/
Adjective
Adjective: slices
Definition

1. Chunks of larger quantity, into smaller, disclosed orders

Related words: slice feeds

Smart Contract

/smart kantrækt/
Adjective
Adjective: smart contract
Definition

1. This is a method using bitcoins to form
   agreement with people through blockchain

Related words: Redistributed contract, Smart
property

SoftFork

/saft fɔrk/
Adjective
Adjective: software
Definition

1. This is a change in the bitcoin protocol in
   which previously valid blocks and
   transactions are made valid since old
   nodes will recognize the new bocks as
   valid.

Related words: Hardfork

Software Wallet

/sɔftwɛr wɔlət/

Adjective

Adjective: software wallet

Definition

1. This refers to a client software used to manage public and private keys and to make transactions on the crypto currency network

Related words: Bitcoin wallet,

Stale Block

/stel blak/

Noun

Noun: stale block

Definition

1. These are blocks which are successfully mined but which are not in the current best block chain because the chain has not been extended yet.

Related words: blocks, orphan block

Standard Deviation

/stændərd diviefən/

Adjectives

Adjectives: standard deviation

Definition

1. This is a statistical term that measures the amount of variability around an average
2. This is the measure of volatility

Related words: Bollinger bands

Stochastic

/stochastics/

Adjective

Adjective: stochastics

1. This is a form of mathematical algorithm used in cryptography

Related words: stochastic indicator

Stochastic Momentum Index

/stochastics momentəm ındɛks /
Adjective
Adjectives: stochastic momentum index
Definition

1. This provides a refinement of the stochastic oscillator
2. This shows the distance of current close relatives to the center of high-low range

Related words: stochastic oscillator

Stop-Loss Order

/stap lɔs ɔrdər /
Adjective
Adjective: stop-loss order
Definition

1. This is a form of sale order that investors often issue when the price of an investment goes below an acceptable loss limit

Related words:

Swing Index

/ swɪŋ ɪndɛks /
Adjective
Adjectives: swing index
Definition

1. This is a technical analysis indicator tool which gives potential short-term buy and sell signal

Relative words: Accumulative Swing index

Symmetrical Triangle

/ səmɛtrɪkəl trajæŋgəl /
Adjectives
Adjectives: symmetrical triangle
Definition

1. This is a chart pattern that is easily recognized by the distinct shape created by two converging trend lines from two sequential lower peaks and a series of two sequential higher troughs.

Related word: triangular pattern

T

Technical Analysis

/tɛknɪkəl ənæləsəs/
Adjectives
Adjectives: technical analysis
Definition

1. This is the use of trading rules, terms, moving averages, regression, and inter-market pricing etc. for graph or chart analysis

Related words:

Timestamp(ing)

/timestamp ɪŋ/
Verb
Verb: timestamping
Definition

1. The use of electronic stamps that shows timing to provide a temporal order among different sets of events;

2. A form of digital signature showing time and date of transactions.

Related words: signature

Token

/tokən/
Noun
Noun: token
Definition

1. This is a technology that helps in the creation of decentralized networks and new ways to incentivize open network participants
2. This is a technology that helps in combining the best architectural properties of open and proprietary networks

Related words: crypto token

Token as a Service

/tokən æz e sərvəs/
Adjectives
Adjective: token as a service
Definition

1. This is an organization building a secure and transparent closed end and fund that enables users to invest in blockchain assets without the risks attached to cryptocurrencies.

Related words:
Abbreviation: TAAS

Timeline

/tajmlajn/
Adjective
Adjective:timeline
Definition

1. A presentation of a chronological sequence of events along a drawn line that enables a viewer to understand temporal relationships quickly
2. Tabular chronology, year by year paragraphs or purely conceptual.

Related words

Trade Volume

/tred valjum/
Adjective
Adjective: trade volume
Definition

1. This is the specified amount of security or market stock traded within a period of time
2. Technical indicator measures the amount of money that flows in and out of an asset

Related words: volume

Trade Volume Index

/tred valjum/
Adjective
Adjective: trade volume index

Definition:

1. This index measures the amount of money that flows in and out of a market;

2. This index identifies if assets are being accumulated or distributed over a period of time.

Abbreviation: TVI
Related words: trading

Trading

/tredɪŋ/
Verb
Verb: trading
Definitions

1. This is the exchange of goods and services or the exchange of commodities using either liquid or digital currency as a medium of exchange.

Related words:

Trading Walls

/tredɪŋ wɔlz/
Adjective
Adjective: trading walls
Definitions

1. This is a wall that represents a temporal high demand in interest either in buying or in selling any kind of digital currency.
2. A trading walls either a buy wall or a sold wall

Related words, bid walls, buy wall, sell wall

Transaction

/trænzækʃən /
Verb
Verb: transaction
Definitions

1. This is an arrangement between a buyer and a seller in order to exchange financial instruments, like cryptocurrencies.

Related words:

Transaction Fee

/trænzækʃən fi/

Adjective

Adjective: transaction fee

Definitions

1. A transaction is processed and received by a bitcoin miner when he or she generates a new bitcoin block with a successful hash
2. This refers to the expense, a person or an organization incurs, each time it processes a transaction through a financial institution.

Related words:

Triangle Pattern

/trajæŋgəl pætərn/

Adjective

Adjective: triangle pattern

Definition

1. This is an analysis pattern on a chart created by drawing trendlines along a price range that gets narrower overdue time low tops and higher bottoms

Related words: Ascending triangle, Descending triangle, and Symmetric Triangle.

Triple Bottom Reversal

/trɪpəl batəm/

Adjective

Adjective: triple bottom reversal

Definitions

1. This is a bullish reversal pattern typically found on a chart

2. This is a formed on a chart when a downward trend in value is being tested by investors

Related words: Triple Top Pattern

Triple Top Reversal

/trɪpəl tap /

Adjectives

Adjectives: triple top reversal

Definitions

1. This is a bearish reversal pattern typically found on market charts

2. This is a pattern that forms on a market chart when investors are testing a bearish trend in value

Related words: Triple Bottom Pattern

Unconfirmed Transaction

/ənkənfərmd trænzækʃən/

Adjective

Adjective: unconfirmed transaction

Definition

1. This means that a transaction or a block of digital currency has not being tagged as unconfirmed based on the fact that supposed transaction fees have not being paid

Related words

Upper Shadow

/əpər ʃædo/

Adjective

Adjective: upper shadow

Definition

1. This represents the highest price, a market stock reaches.

Related words: upper wick

Uptrend

/əptrɛnd /

Adjective

Adjective: uptrend

1. This is a price movement of a financial asset when the overall direction is upward.

2. This is movement in the chart showing an uptrend in which each successive peak and trough is higher than the ones found earlier in the trend

Related words: Downtrend.

V

Value

/ vælju /
Adjective
Adjective: value
Definition

1. The regard or worth a commodity, virtual currency is held to deserve.

2. The productivity of a commodity

Related words: worth

Verified Transaction

/ vɛrəfajd trænzækʃən /
Adjective
Adjective: verified transaction
Definition

1. A sworn or certified transaction

2. This is a transaction that has passed all terms and conditions of certification and is recorded

Related words: certified transaction

Virgin Coin
/ vərdʒən kɔjn /
Noun
Noun: virgin coin
Definitions

1. This refers to coin that not being transferred from their initial mining wallet
2. This also means newly generated coins

Related words; Satoshi, BTC

Volume Adjusted Moving Average
/valjum ədʒəstəd muvɪŋ ævərɪdʒ /
Adjective
Adjective: volume adjusted moving averages
Definition

1. This is a moving average that takes into account the volume of single days and time periods, in computing price averages
2. This makes price volume equal partners in computing the price average

Related word: equivolume chart

Vol Underlay

/ vol underlay /
Adjectives
Adjectives: vol underlay
Definition

1. This is a technical analysis indicator which simply displays the total volume as a bar chart each of the chart periods

Related words: volumes, charts

Volume

/ valjum /
Adjective
Adjective volume
Definition

1. A technical analysis indicator that displays the totality of a volume as a bar chart aligning with each of the chart's periods

Relative words: volume underlay, volume oscillator.

Volume Oscillator

/valjum asəletər /
Adjective
Adjective: volume oscillator
Definition

1. The volume oscillator displays the difference between to different moving averages of a securities volume which varies in short term period, long term periods etc.

Related words: volume underlay

Volume Rate of Change

/ valjum ret əv tʃendʒ /
Adjective
Adjective: volume rate of change
Definition

1. This is a technical indicator measure the rate of change in the volume over a period of time.

Related words: volume oscillator

Wallet (Secure/Not Secure)
/ wɔlət /
Adjective
Adjective: wallet
definition

1. This is something that stores the digital credentials for your virtual currencies thereby providing access to sending and receiving more currencies
2. This is a collection of private keys in a web or software program used to manage such keys and make viral transactions

Related words: hardware wallet, software.

Web Wallet
/ wɛb wɔlət /
Adjective
Adjective: web wallet
Definition

1. This is a web program where cryptocurrencies are stored
2. A browser based wallet with an online account wit and service provider who stores virtual currency

Related words: wallet

Wedge Pattern

/wɛdʒ pætərn /
Adjective
Adjective: wedge pattern
Definition

1. This a technical indicator which signals a reverse in the web of trends that is being formed within the wedge itself.

Related words: symmetric triangle

Whales

/ welz /
Noun
Noun: whale
Definition

1. This is a bitcoin big money player that is present in the bitcoin market
2. Large players in the market being referred to as institutions.

Related words: ocean

White Paper
/wajt pepər /
Noun
Noun: white paper
Definition

1. A white paper is a term that describes the blockchain technology and some compelling scientific application in the financial and non-financial sector.

Related words

William %R
/ wɪljəm ar /
Noun
Noun: William %R
Definition

1. This is a momentum indicator that is used to measure overbought and oversold level comparable to a stochastic oscillator

Acronyms: William percentage range
Related words:

Withdrawal

/ wəðdrɔəl /

Verb

Verb: withdrawal

Definition

1. This refers involves removing funds from a financial institution or an investment
2. Removal of assets in cash or in kind

Related word: cash

X11 Mining

/ x11 majnɪŋ /
Adjective
Adjective: x11 mining
Definition

1. This is a widely used hashing algorithm approach that utilizes a sequence of eleven scientific hashing algorithms for proof of work

Related words: x15 mining, x13 mining.

X13 Mining

/X13 majnɪŋ /
Adjective
Adjectives: x13 mining
Definition

1. This is a widely used hashing algorithm approach that utilizes a sequence of thirteen scientific hashing algorithms for proof of work

Related words: x14 mining, X13mining

X15 Mining
/ majnɪŋ x15 /
Adjective
Adjective: x15 mining
Definition

1. This is a widely used hashing algorithm approach that utilizes a sequence of fifteen scientific hashing algorithms for proof of work

Related words: x14 mining, x13 mining, x11mining

XBP
/xbps/
Adjective
Adjective: xbp
Definition

1. XBP indicator is a technical analysis tool used in analyzing the set of market by price volume and tape action

Related words: oscillator

Z

Zero Confirmation Transaction

/ zɪro kanfərmeʃən trænzækʃən /
Adjective
Adjective: zero confirmation transaction
Definition

1. This refers to the immediate verification of transaction process without waiting for confirmation of a data block.

Related words

Printed in Great Britain
by Amazon